HOMEMADE KETO SALAD DRESSING

SPICY VEGETARIAN KETO SALAD BOOK

By

Laura Marvin

Acknowledgement

I never believed I could make this book come to reality, but with the support of friends, family members and colleagues, this dream is fulfilled! I remain forever indebted to you all for your encouragement and support.

Special thanks to Alicia, a close friend and more like a sister for her help in making deep research about the contents of this wonderful book. Your ideas polished my culinary skills and gave birth to this book.

To my lovely family, I can never do without you. The Keto diet has been changing life, and I'm glad to have the opportunity to make contributions and help change the lives of many, especially those looking to lose weight through the keto way of life!

Introduction

How can I lose weight fast?

This particular question has been asked so many times, and it is popularly believed that you lose more weight by burning more calories. You may be wondering if the spicy keto vegetarian salads in this cookbook can help you lose weight, but how can you be sure?

What if I tell you that you can lose weight by eating more? Sounds crazy right? Well, it shouldn't, as this is exactly what the keto diet does. You don't have to go hungry all day starving yourself or even be fasting. With the keto diet, you can lose weight even as you eat more.

Yes, contrary to what many believed, fat is the secret! It is what makes the keto diet work. Even though you need to consume more fat to live a keto lifestyle, have it at the back of your mind that what you need is heathy fat. So how do you know which meal to eat? Which fat is healthy?

You aren't the only one, these questions has been going through the mind of many who haven't tried keto diet or understand what it truly is. This is why we are here for you. With this cookbook, you don't have to worry about selecting healthy fats or keto foods. Since you have made up your mind to live the keto lifestyle, this cookbook is here to guide you in selecting yummy low-carb keto vegetarian salads. Sit back as we talk about the keto concept and how it works!

Basics of a Keto Diet to Help You Feel & Look Better

The pursuit of weight loss is the reason many are leaving behind their current unhealthy lifestyle and adapting different eating patterns. Many people have seen the way certain diets helps them lose weight, and one of such is the keto diet. How then does the keto diet helps you lose weight?

What is Ketosis?

Starting out on the keto diet is very essential, but as a beginner you may not be familiar with the terms associated with it. To begin with, beginners usually ask, 'what is ketosis?' This question shows that you really want to change your diet and work on your overall health. Well, in simplified terms, ketosis means the state where your body no longer relies on sugar for energy, but rather relies on ketone bodies for energy. This shouldn't confuse you, as it is very simple.

To break it further down...

The major sources of energy for your body is fat and sugar (popularly known as glucose).

The main aim of a ketogenic diet (also known as ketosis or keto diet), is to burn more fat and convert it to energy, rather than glucose.

How are ketone bodies produced?

Ketones are formed by the liver when fat is broken down by the body. Your body enters into a state of metabolism known as ketosis when there is an improved level of ketone bodies in your blood.

What should I include in my ketogenic diet?

Your keto diet should consists of foods that improves ketosis. Simply put, you should consume less sugar or carbs while eating plenty healthy fats. Yes, healthy fats, and not just any type of fats. In your keto diet, let your consumption of protein be moderate. What this is pointing to is that you should consume foods that don't increase your blood sugar level that much, meaning you should consume only low-'glycemic' foods.

If you follow this diet pattern, your body will get the signal and be forced to begin using up fat to generate energy, rather than just sugar.

This process helps your body to be able to draw energy from various sources, not just sugar. It means that you have gained metabolic flexibility. Your body drawing energy from different sources is god for your overall wellbeing, as you will become more energetic, have improved mental alertness, and of course, loss weight!

Because of its success, the keto diet has been around for so long with more and more people adapting to it. When it all began, the main aim was to combat epilepsy in kids, and surprisingly, this has shown to have many other benefits, especially weight loss.

What can keto diet do for you?

Here are surprising benefits of keto diet

Many researches are done about the keto diet, and from these studies, researchers are amazed at the benefits of keto diet, and various studies indicate that it can help battle cancer and diseases affecting the nervous system. Keto diet is also helpful for weight loss and also to combat diabetes. Without wasting much time, here is a collection of what keto diet can do for you:

1- Lowers the risk of High Cholesterol and Triglycerides

Typically, a diet rich in fat can increase cholesterol, but with keto diet, it is different. Filled with healthy fats, keto diets helps significantly reduce cholesterol and triglycerides levels in most people.

2- Weight loss

This is the main reason many people have adopted the keto diet. Although it doesn't happen magically overnight, people tend to lose weight faster and easier when on a keto diet. To back this up, keto diet assists in hunger reduction, thus helping you lose weight. Switching to a keto diet isn't something you just stumble upon, you should be highly prepared because it isn't easy sticking to a keto diet.

3- Helps in combating certain cancer types

Keto has the potential of battling cancer, as many researches have shown that it can fight against certain types of cancer, most especially brain cancer, particularly when used together with other forms of traditional treatments.

4- Reducing high blood sugar levels

Since keto is all about replacing sugar with healthy fat, it obviously helps reduce high blood sugar level and is good for diabetics, helping promote healthy blood sugar levels.

5- Reduces hunger

In most diet types, you have to focus more on your willpower, restricting portions and even counting calories. However, the keto diet is different, since it forces your body to begin using more of healthy fats rather than sugar to generate energy, making your hunger reduce and forces you to eat less.

6- Helps fight Neurological Disorders

In its early stages, the Keto diet was used just to treat epilepsy. Today, there are other neurological disorders that are treated with keto diet, especially Alzheimer's disease.

Keto diet has many other potentials, and many studies are indicating that keto diet can treat other conditions like PCOS, acne, and respiratory conditions amongst others.

How much nutrient should you take to get into ketosis?

It differs from person to person, and the exact number of nutrients, be it fat, protein and carbs to take for you to enter ketosis varies. However, let's throw in some general recommendations.

For carbohydrate, you should not consume more than 20-25 grams of net carbs daily especially if your keto diet is targeted at weight loss or if you have insulin sensitivity. However, athletes are advised to add more carbs, but it should be at least under 100g daily.

For protein, you have to get it right, as too little or too many can negatively affect ketosis. You should multiply your weight (in lbs.) by 0.6 for the minimum, and by 1.0 for the maximum daily protein intake in grams. This is because if you take too little protein, then lean muscle tissue can be compromised, and if you take too much protein, ketone production can be reduced. With this, if for example you weigh 110 lbs., then your medium protein intake should be 110 x 0.6 = 66 grams, while maximum should be 110 x 1 = 110 grams.

Ketosis is all about consuming healthy fats. For this reason, you should include more heathy fats in your diet such as olive oil, coconut oil, animal fats, avocado oil, and ghee, amongst others. Overall, your fat intake should be more than that of protein and especially carbs.

Whatever you eat, remember that much of your calories should come from healthy high fat foods and very little from carbs.

I believe that by now, you must have grabbed a better understanding of what the ketogenic diet is all about. Now, get ready, we present to you mouthwatering low carb keto vegetarian salads!

Vegetarian salads

Salads are made to complete your meals, and these vegetarian salads surely will fill you up!

Low-carb zucchini and walnut salad

Time to prepare: ten (10) minutes

Time to cook: five (5) minutes

Difficulty level: Easy

This nutty low-carb salad is crunchy and blessed with the flavor of sautéed Zucchini. Enjoy this yummy treat!

Ingredients you will need:

- ¼ cup finely chopped fresh chives or scallions

- salt and pepper

- 1 tbsp. olive oil

- 1 head of Romaine lettuce

- ¾ cup chopped walnuts or pecans

- 4 oz. arugula lettuce

- 2 zucchini

For the dressing:

- 1 garlic clove

- 2 tbsp. olive oil

- ¼ tsp chili powder

- 2 tsp lemon juice

- ¾ cup mayonnaise

- ½ tsp salt

How to prepare

1- Mix together in a small bowl all ingredients for the dressing. Keep the dressing separate for some time to develop flavor, and use this time to prepare the salad.

2- Cut the zucchini length-wise and scrub out the seeds. Into ½-inch pieces split the zucchini halves crosswise.

3- In a frying pan, until it sparkles, heat olive oil over medium heat. Now, to the pan, add zucchini, and use salt and pepper to season. Stir fry until it becomes lightly browned while still firm.

4- Trim the salad, then cut it. Place, in a large bowl, the arugula, romaine, and chives. Add in the cooked zucchini and stir.

5- Quickly roast the nuts in the same pan with the zucchini. Use salt and pepper to season. Finally, onto salad, spoon the nuts and sprinkle with salad dressing.

Useful advice:

You can tryout different combinations as the dressing can be used with other salads, or even used as a tasty sauce for fish or meat. You can make extra dressing since it can be stored for at least five days in the fridge. Even the zucchini salad can be used with other meals.

Roasted fennel and snow pea salad

Time to Prepare: five (5) minutes

Time to Cook: thirty (30) minutes

Difficulty level: Easy

This low carb salad is loved by many who have made it their favorite. It tastes great and even greater when served with pumpkin seeds and snow peas.

Ingredients you will need:

- 3 tbsp. olive oil

- 51⁄3 oz. snow peas

- sea salt

- 1 lemon

- ground black pepper

- 1 lb. fresh fennel

- 2 tbsp. sunflower seeds or pumpkin seeds, toasted

How to prepare:

1-   To 450°F (225°C) preheat the oven.

2-   Into little wedges, cut the fennel. In a baking dish, get it arranged. Sprinkle olive oil on top, then to taste, add salt and pepper.

3-   In two, cut the lemon and then crush out the juice and keep it safe for future usage. Into thin wedges, slice the lemon rind and spread around the fennel (you will get better flavor with oven-baked lemon, but you can skip if you don't like eating them).

4-   Bake for twenty (20) – thirty (30) minutes in the oven or when the fennel has transformed into a nice golden color.

5-   In a dry frying pan, put the pumpkin seeds while the fennel is still baking, then, for a few minutes, toast over medium heat until it starts becoming brown but not burnt.

6-   With the dry toasted pumpkin seeds and raw shredded snow peas, mix the roasted fennel. Dish out in a plate and serve.

Useful advice:

Don't throw away the fronds and fennel stalks after you cut them because you can eat the fronds raw and use the stalks in soup stalks. Yummy!

Oriental red cabbage salad

Time to prepare: five (5) minutes

Time to cook: twenty (20) minutes

Difficulty level: easy

Create a superb side dish with a combination of orange, fresh cinnamon, and dill mixed with shredded red cabbage! This refreshing side is light and have beautiful colors, suitable for holidays and other times.

Ingredients you will need:

- 2 tbsp. fresh dill, chopped

- 4¼ oz. butter

- ¼ tsp ground black pepper

- 1 tsp salt

- 30 oz. red cabbage

- 1 tbsp. red wine vinegar

- 1 cinnamon stick

- 1 orange, juice and zest

How to prepare:

1. In a food processor or a mandolin slicer, thinly shred the cabbage.

2. On medium high fry in butter for ten (10) – fifteen (15) minutes. Gently fry the

cabbage until it becomes shiny and soft, but not too brown.

3.   Add pepper and salt. Pour in orange juice, vinegar, and cinnamon. Allow it to cook for five (5) – ten (10) minutes.

4.   Finally, top with zest and dill when serving or towards the end.

Useful advice:

Use any leftover as a topping on a sandwich and enjoy!

Oven-roasted Brussels sprouts with parmesan cheese

Time to prepare: ten (10) minutes

Time to cook: twenty (20) minutes

Difficulty level: easy

Brussels sprouts are awesome and yummy when roasted with olive oil in the oven.

Ingredients you will need:

- 3 tbsp. olive oil

- salt and pepper

- 1 tsp dried rosemary or dried thyme

- 20 oz. Brussels sprouts

- 3 oz. shaved parmesan cheese

How to prepare:

1-   To 450°F (225°C), preheat the oven.

2-   Get the Brussels sprouts trimmed and have them divided in two equal parts.

3-   Now, transfer in a baking dish, and add olive oil on top. Also add pepper and salt and also add thyme or rosemary.

4-   Roast for 15–20 minutes in the oven or when the Brussels sprouts have transformed into a pleasant color. Add the parmesan cheese and enjoy!

Useful advice:

It is advisable to use fresh Brussels sprouts for oven-roasted Brussel sprouts. If you have only frozen Brussels sprouts, then it is better to have them lightly boiled and in a frying pan, using spices and oil, have them quickly fried. When serving you can add the parmesan cheese.

Simple keto coleslaw

Time to prepare: ten (10) minutes

Difficulty level: easy

Coleslaw, a favorite keto side dish is good for all meals. It is easy to make, and also tasty too!

Ingredients you will need:

- 1 cup mayonnaise
- ¼ tsp ground black pepper
- ½ tsp salt
- 15 oz. green cabbage

How to prepare:

1. In a food processor, with a sharp knife, or mandolin slicer shred the cabbage.

2. Transfer to a bowl and add salt, mayonnaise and pepper. Properly stir and allow it to settle for ten (10) minutes.

Useful advice:

You can spice things up by splashing lemon or vinegar. Since coleslaw can last for three (3) to four (4) days in the fridge, you can make a big batch.

Coleslaw

Time to prepare: five (5) minutes

Time to cook: ten (10) minutes

Difficulty level: Easy

Coleslaw, a very popular cabbage salad is loved by many. With a delicious taste, it is complete and can be used with various foods

Ingredients you will need

- 1 pinch pepper
- 1 tbsp. Dijon mustard
- ½ lemon, the juice
- ½ cup mayonnaise

- 1 tsp salt

- ½ lb. green cabbage

- 1 pinch fennel seeds (optional)

How to prepare:

1- Take off the core and using a sharp cheese slicer, mandolin or food processor shred the cabbage.

2- In a medium sized bowl, put the cabbage.

3- Now, add in salt and the lemon juice.

4-   Stir and allow it to rest for ten (10) minutes to make the cabbage wither a little. Do away with any excess liquid.

5-   Now combine cabbage, mayonnaise and optional mustard.

6- To taste, season.

Useful advice:

You can try this same recipe but rather with thin celery root rods or fennel which has been pre-cooked for some minutes in lightly salted water. This too is yummy!

When kept in the fridge, the coleslaw can last for two (2) – three (3) days.

Low-carb fried kale and broccoli salad

Time to prepare: five (5) minutes

Time to cook: fifteen (15) minutes

Difficulty level: easy

You will surely fall in love with this low carb broccoli salad. A combination of garlic, tasty fried kale, creamy avocado and tangy mustard gives you this heavenly delight!

Ingredients you will need:

- 2 tbsp. olive oil

- 1 tbsp. whole-grain mustard

- 4 oz. kale

- ½ lb. broccoli

- ½ cup mayonnaise

- 2 scallions

- 1 pinch chili flakes

- 2 garlic cloves

- salt or pepper to taste

- 2 avocados

- 4 eggs

How to prepare:

1- In a small bowl, mix mustard and mayo and then keep aside.

2- Boil the eggs to your preference, be it soft, medium or even hard-boiled. When they're done, place them in ice cold water Immediately, as this will make them easy for peeling. When they become cool have them divided into two equal parts or quarters.

3- Get the avocados divided, take out the pit and slice them up into bits.

4- Thinly slice the garlic. In a frying pan, heat the oil and with care, fry the garlic slices. From the pan, take out the garlic and transfer to a paper towel for it to become crispy. In the pan, save the oil.

5- Thoroughly chop the kale and broccoli. To the garlic-infused oil in the pan, add a scoop of butter. Now, on medium high heat, for some minutes, fry the vegetables until it become a little bit softened.

6- Finally, use salt and pepper to season, and dish with eggs, avocado, and the mustard mayo. For extra flavor and crunch, use fried garlic slices to complete the dish.

Useful advice:

With baby kale or spinach, greens become very soft. Ensure you purchase them pre-washed to save you time when preparing.

Zucchini salad

Time to prepare: Five (5) minutes

Time to cook: Fifteen (15) minutes

Difficulty level: Easy

Zucchini salad is creamy in flavor, a perfect make for picnics.

Ingredients you will need:

- 2 tbsp. fresh chives, finely chopped

- 2 tbsp. butter or olive oil

- ½ tbsp. Dijon mustard

- salt and pepper

- 1 cup mayonnaise

- 3 oz. celery stalks, finely sliced

- 2 lbs. zucchini

- 2 oz. chopped scallions

How to prepare:

1. Peel, then, into pieces, cut the zucchini, about half an inch (1-1.5 cm) in thickness. Remove the seeds with a spoon. Add in a colander then sprinkle in salt. Let it settle for about five (5) to ten (10) minutes, then with great care, press out the water.

2. Over medium heat, in butter, fry the cubes for some of minutes. Don't let them get brown, let them be slightly soften. keep aside to let it cool.

3.   In a large bowl, combine together the other ingredients and then add the zucchini when it becomes cool.

Useful advice:

Since the flavors enhances with time, you can get the salad ready a day or two ahead of time.

Crispy Brussels sprout salad with lemon

Time to prepare: Ten (10) minutes

Time to cook: Ten (10) minutes

Difficulty level: Easy

Filled with flavor, the fresh Brussels sprouts is garnished with fresh lemon dressing and crunchy almond with seed mixture. You won't regret a taste!

Ingredients you will need:

- ½ cup olive oil

- salt and pepper

- 1 lemon, juice and zest

- 1 lb. Brussels sprouts

-   2⁄5 - ¾ cup spicy almond & a mixture
    of seed or nuts and seeds you prefer

For the Spicy almond and seed mix:

-   2 oz. almonds

-   1 tsp chili paste

-   1 oz. pumpkin seeds

-   1 tbsp. coconut oil or olive oil

-   1 oz. sunflower seeds

-   1 pinch salt

-   ½ tsp ground cumin or crushed fennel
seeds

How to prepare:

1. Thinly cut and rinse the Brussels sprouts. In a food processor or using a sharp knife, shred it roughly. Transfer to a salad bowl.

2. Combine together lemon juice/zest, olive oil, pepper and salt. Sprinkle over the Brussels sprouts.

3. For 10 minutes, allow it to soak. Now, pour in the spicy almond & seed mix straightaway before serving.

4. Use this salad as a side dish for meal of your choice.

For the Spicy almond & seed mix:

1. In a large frying pan, heat the oil, then firstly, add the chili.

2. Now add seeds and almonds then thoroughly stir.

3. Add salt and stir fry for some extra minutes, but be watchful as almonds and seeds are highly sensitive to heat. Make the oil very hot enough to bring out the spice flavors, however the seeds and almonds should not be burnt.

4. Allow it to cool and before serving, sprinkle over the salad.

Useful advice:

To make things quicker, get pre-shredded Brussels sprouts from the market.

Keto kohlslaw

Time to prepare: Ten (10) minutes

Time to cook: Five (5) minutes

Difficulty level: Easy

This may appear strange to you, but don't be discouraged as this low carb veggie is full of vitamins. As refreshing and crisp that it is, it is also light!

Ingredients you will need:

- salt and pepper

- 1 cup mayonnaise

- 15 oz. kohlrabies

- fresh parsley (optional)

How to prepare:

1. Peel the kohlrabi. Make sure that you remove and cut away any part that is tough or woody. Thinly slice, shave, or shred it, then transfer it to a bowl.

2. Add in the mayonnaise and optional fresh herbs, then sprinkle pepper and salt to taste.

Useful advice:

Even though Kohlrabi is mostly found at farmer's market, you can still get it at your local super market most likely from the produce section. A paring knife or peeler can be used for peeling it, and you should take away the woody exterior. You will now be left without fibers, only light green / white. This versatile vegetable can also be used raw in salads, roasted like potatoes and can serve as a substitute for cabbage in different recipes.

Warm keto kale salad

Time to prepare: ten (10) minutes

Time to cook: ten (10) minutes

Difficulty level: easy

This warm keto salad is outstanding! You can use it as a side dish for your meals. Enjoy!

Ingredients you will need:
-   2 tbsp. mayonnaise

- 2 tbsp. olive oil

- 1 tsp Dijon mustard

- ¾ cup heavy whipping cream

- salt and pepper

- 4 oz. blue cheese or feta cheese

- 2 oz. butter

- 1 garlic clove, minced or finely chopped

- 8 oz. kale

How to prepare:

1. In a small beaker, combine mayonnaise, heavy cream, mustard, garlic and olive oil. Then to taste, add pepper and salt.

2. Rinse the kale then slice into little, chewable pieces. Do away with the thick stem.

3. Get a large frying pan heated and add the butter. Quickly stir fry the kale so it transforms into a nice color, but don't leave it any longer. To taste, add salt and pepper.

4. Transfer into a bowl and on top, pour the dressing. Vigorously stir and serve as you prefer.

Useful advice:

You can use this dressing with any type of leafy green salad. To make green juice, keep the kale stems and ribs. Save them for use in making juice!

Caprese snack

Time to prepare: five (5) minutes

Difficulty level: Easy

Decorate your plate with delicious treats, pleasant to the eyes and with sweet aroma. With this Caprese your plate is filled with nice colors that are good to behold, sweet aroma and makes you instantly hungry. It can serve as a side or as an appetizer.

Ingredients you will need:
- 8 oz. mozzarella, mini cheese balls
- 8 oz. cherry tomatoes
- salt and pepper
- 2 tbsp. green pesto

How to prepare:

1- In two equal parts cut the tomatoes and mozzarella balls. Now put in pesto and stir.

2- Finally, for taste, add salt and pepper.

Useful advice:

When you add parsley, fresh basil, or chives, you can make the Caprese more appetizing!

Mixed cabbage coleslaw

Time to prepare: Ten (10) minutes

Difficulty level: Easy

This quick and easy side dish is fresh, light and colorful too. Enjoy it for block parties, picnics and anytime you wish!

Ingredients you will need:

- ¼ tsp ground black pepper

- 4 oz. red cabbage

- ½ tsp salt

- 4 oz. kale

- 8 oz. green cabbage

- 1 cup mayonnaise

How to prepare:

1. Using a sharp knife, mandolin slicer or a food processor, cut the cabbage into pieces.

2. Transfer into a bowl and add the mayonnaise, pepper and salt. Properly stir it and give it ten (10) minutes for it to settle.

Useful advice:

You can keep the remaining refrigerated for about three (3) to four (4) days when you make a big batch.

Eggplant salad

Time to prepare: Fifteen (15) minutes

Time to cook: Thirty (30) minutes

Difficulty level: Medium

The aroma from grilled eggplant and bell peppers will leave you hungry and is good for winter!

Ingredients you will need:

- 2 garlic cloves

- 2 eggplant

- 1 tsp salt

- 1 red chili pepper

- 1 lemon, the juice

- ½ cup mayonnaise

- 2 green bell peppers

- ½ cup fresh parsley

How to prepare:

1. To 480°F (250°C), get the oven preheated.

2. In half length-wise, cut the eggplants and bell peppers and seed the bell peppers.

3. In an ovenproof dish, place the vegetables peel-side up.

4. In the middle of the oven, place the dish and for half an hour, bake, and as you do,

after every twenty minutes, turn the eggplants.

5. from the oven, take down the dish and let the vegetables cool down a little.

6. In half, cut the chili and seed it. NOTE: make use of rubber gloves to carry out this task, and no matter how tempting, DO NOT touch your face!

7. You can leave the seeds in if you want an eggplant salad that is much more spicy.

8. Finely chop the chili.

9. Now, slice the parsley and have the garlic crushed.

10. Combine and mix everything in a bowl with the lemon juice.

11. Take off the skins from the grilled vegetables and slice them into tiny dices, then add to the mayonnaise and parsley mix.

12. Mix it thoroughly.

13. Give it a few hours to chill as this makes the flavor develop strongly.

Creamy turnip slaw

Time to prepare: ten (10) minutes

Difficulty level: easy

This alternative method of preparing coleslaw is a wonderful side featuring turnip at the center stage!

Ingredients you will need:

- 15 oz. turnip

- 1 tbsp. cider vinegar

- 1 small carrot or apple (optional)

- 1⁄3 cup fresh parsley or fresh coriander or fresh mint finely chopped

- 1 cup mayonnaise

- salt and pepper

How to prepare:

1. Thoroughly rinse the vegetables then peel. For the apple, instead of peeling, just core it. In a machine or by hand, grate everything into rough pieces, then transfer to a bowl.

2. Put in all the remaining ingredients, then mix to combine. Season to taste.

3. Finally, serve as a fresh side dish.

Useful advice:

Instead of using the turnip, you can substitute it for the stem of broccoli, kohlrabi or black radish.

Roasted tomato salad

Time to prepare: five (5) minutes

Time to cook: twenty (20) minutes

Difficulty level: easy

With a nice summer taste, these sweet roasted cherry tomatoes have the right taste and is good to try out!

Ingredients you will need:

- 1 tbsp. red wine vinegar

- 1 tsp sea salt

- 3 tbsp. olive oil

- ½ tsp ground black pepper

- 1 lb. cherry tomatoes

- ½ cup finely chopped scallions

How to prepare:

1. With oil, brush the tomatoes to cover, then with spices, sprinkle.

2. Cook on top of the grill, with the use of a special vegetable accessory, or in the oven until the tomatoes have become a little bit browned.

3. If the oven is what you are using, bake for about 15 minutes at 450°F (225°C). Stir and put off the oven, but allow the tomatoes to bake for an extra time, about ten (10) more minutes.

4. Transfer to a plate, then on top, sprinkle chopped scallions. Use vinegar and the remaining olive oil to drizzle. Give it time to rest so that the flavors mix properly, and finally, serve the salad either lukewarm or cold.

Useful advice:

If you like a salad that is more salsa-like, vigorously slice the tomatoes in rough pieces. You can add in some crushed feta for added flavor. It serves as an awesome side for virtually anything grilled and great for summer time!

Red coleslaw

Time to prepare: Ten (10) minutes

Difficulty level: Easy

A sweet alternative to the usual one, this amazing keto dish is awesome for winter holidays.

Ingredients you will need:

- 1 tbsp. whole-grain mustard

- 1¼ cups mayonnaise

- 12⁄3 lbs. red cabbage

- ¼ tsp ground black pepper

- 1 tsp salt

- 2 tsp ground caraway seeds

How to prepare:

1. In a food processor or making use of a mandolin slicer, thinly shred the cabbage.

2. Combine together with other ingredients and give it about 10–15 minutes before you serve.

Useful advice:

Do you have left over shredded cabbage? No worries! Transfer it into a tightly closed plastic bag and refrigerate for several days. You can use it for another recipe.

Broccoli salad with fresh dill

Time to prepare: Five (5) minutes

Time to cook: Five (5) minutes

Difficulty level: Easy

Special Broccoli, all for you. This delicious natural super veggie is a tasty side dish. Broccoli combined with fresh dill is deliciously tasty!

Ingredients you will need:

- 1 lb. broccoli

- ¾ cup fresh dill

- 1 cup mayonnaise

- salt and ground black pepper to taste

1- Into little buds, slice the broccoli and the stalks into more thinner pieces. To boiling salted water, add the floret pieces and the stalks and allow it to boil for about four (4) to five (5) minutes. Let the broccoli be bright green and fork tender without losing its crispness.

2- Drain the broccoli then add the other ingredients and stir. Season with pepper. If necessary, adjust with more salt.

Useful advice:

You can use cauliflower or halved Brussels sprouts in place of the broccoli. In addition, you can use frozen veggies, and even if the texture is a bit different, all the nutrients are still intact!

Greek salad

Time to prepare: Ten (10) minutes

Difficulty level: Easy

Greek style is awesome, especially with this classic salad which is a low carb naturally. Loved by the Greeks, this side is naturally delicious.

Ingredients you will need:

- 3 ripe tomatoes

- 2 tsp dried oregano

- ½ red onion

- ½ tbsp. red wine vinegar

- ½ green bell pepper

- salt and pepper

- 7 oz. feta cheese

- 4 tbsp. olive oil

- 10 black Greek olives

- ½ cucumber

How to prepare:

1. Into chewable sized pieces, slice the cucumber and tomatoes. Finely slice the onion and the bell pepper. Get it arranged on a serving tray or, if possible, dish the salad on separate salad plates.

2. Add olives and feta cheese, then over the salad, sprinkle vinegar and olive oil.

3. As desired, season with salt and pepper to taste. Finally, drizzle with crumbled oregano and serve.

Useful advice:

For a different appearance, you can try cherry tomatoes or swap the colors. You can even crumble the fetta for a different presentation.